A National Park Service Historic Structures Report

The Moore House

The Site of the Surrender—Yorktown

Charles E. Peterson

NPCA
PUBLICATION

A National Parks & Conservation Association Publication

Cover illustration: Pencil sketch of the Moore House,
Temple Farm, Colonial National Historical Park by Charles E. Peterson
1930/1. Original presented to the late Congressman Louis C. Cramton
of Michigan.

A National Park Service Historic Structures Report

Published by:
National Parks & Conservation Association
1701 18th Street, N.W.
Washington, D.C. 20009

Manufactured in the United States of America

CONTENTS

FOREWORD

A s we observe the 200th anniversary of the victory at Yorktown and the conclusion of the Revolutionary War, it is also appropriate that we mark the first publication of the 1935 report about the restoration of the Moore House, made famous by the surrender of Lord Cornwallis to General Washington and the Allied French Forces.

The Moore House was the first historic building to be restored by the National Park Service, and this report by Charles E. Peterson was the progenitor of all Historic Structures Reports prepared by the National Park Service during the past 50 years. It is a significant document in the history of the American preservation movement.

This report combined the then known facts relating to the physical evolution of the house, together with mention of the ''commemorative'' work carried out by the Yorktown Centennial Association for Centennial observances in 1881. The report also described the work carried out by the National Park Service architects in the few weeks before the great Sesqui-Centennial Celebration of October 1931; and soon afterwards, as more old views of the house came to light, it was possible to incorporate the discoveries in further work completed in 1934. This report marks the first real attempt at accountability of the scholarship and the architectural investigation involved in an historic building restoration.

The National Park Service deeply appreciates the friendly gesture of the National Parks and Conservation Association in publishing this report from the original typescript in time for distribution at the Bicentennial Celebration.

> Russell E. Dickenson
> Director, National Park Service

Washington, September 1981

National Parks & Conservation Association is a private, non-profit citizen association seeking to establish and maintain the world's first and finest park system. This publication is part of our educational role to inform the public of the heritage of our parks and the relationship of elements within the park to the story of that park. Moore House was the setting for a very significant event in our nation's history. National park preservation has maintained that structure for us today. And, Charles Peterson has assured us that it will be protected accurately.

The National Parks & Conservation Association is pleased to publish this time honored publication of Charles Peterson and the National Park Service.

Gilbert F. Stucker   Paul C. Pritchard
Chairman   Executive Director
Board of Trustees

September, 1981

THE MOORE HOUSE REPORT:
A RETROSPECTIVE

The Moore House Report is not only the "grandfather" of all Historic Structures Reports for the National Park Service, but it marks the Service's entry into historic preservation in the early 1930's. Quite apart from its remarkable prescient quality as a fully developed model with few if any predecessors, it was Peterson's own views regarding the purpose of the report and the stewardship responsibility of the restoration architect that mark this report as a milestone in the American preservation movement. There is an important underlying philosophy very ably expressed in Peterson's own words which bear repeating here:

> It is my opinion that any architect who undertakes the responsibility of working over a fine old building should feel obligated to prepare a detailed report of his findings for the information of those who will come to study it in future years. Such a volume should become a permanent part of the building—a payment by the architect for the privilege of learning and using facts which no other man may ever have.

Since the Moore House, hundreds of restoration projects have been carried out resulting in thousands of Historic Structures Reports involving the research and investigations of historians, architects, and archeologists. Over the years, these reports have evolved through a number of formats to suit changing professional and administrative needs, but there are certain types of information that are common to most if not all such reports.

A Historic Structures Report, first defined by the Moore House Report in 1935, is usually a compendium of all known information about the historic structure, and includes documents such as letters, photographs, drawings, etc., together with the results of archeological and architectural investigations, to better understand the building, its evolution and present condition.

The public is little aware of the role of such reports in the National Park Service's preservation programs, since virtually none of these reports have ever been published. These reports are prepared, when needed, at the planning stage, after completion of research, and upon completion of the project. The reports present the conclusions of the investigators and researchers regarding the physical evolution and condition of the building and recommend plans for preservation, rehabilitation and restoration.

Over the years, this writer has read hundreds of historic structures reports, and has been involved in the preparation of many such reports, either personally or in collaboration with other professionals; but despite the ever growing body of knowledge and complexities revealed in today's historic structures reports, they all share the common thrust and context of accountability represented by Charles E. Peterson's Moore House Report.

There will be those who will fault the apparent haste and conjecture involved in the Moore House restoration. Such perceptions, in the opinion of this writer, lack the historic understanding of that remarkable and embryonic period that produced Colonial Williamsburg (in the private sector) and the creation of Colonial National Historic Park (in the Federal sector). The relationship between these two creations, and an account of the National Park Service entry into the "historic park field" (a Horace Albright term) can be found in Charles B. Hosmer, Jr., *Preservation Comes of Age*, volume 1, Charlottesville, 1981.

This writer has seen most of the "early" reports of historical researches and investigations involving historic buildings, including those of Colonial Williamsburg, and I can assure you that Peterson's report is in a class by itself, not because it is better researched (it isn't), or because it is a better restoration (it had the same "brilliant" architects, Perry, Shaw, and Hepburn), but because the accountability concept produced a remarkably complete report for use in interpreting the restoration to the public. The report included all known early views, an assessment of the physical evolution, citations relating to sources of conjectural details, and accounts of the government activities including archeology, physical investigation, and descriptions of "corrective" work (indicating the commitment to accuracy). A detailed set of measured drawings of the house was made when the work was first underway in the Spring of 1931; and when the Historic American Buildings Survey (H.A.B.S.) was established two years later, the drawings were retraced on the H.A.B.S. format for the Library of Congress collection, and copies were included as a part of the Moore House Report.

Peterson's report reveals many details relating to the events and individual contributions to the Moore House era, but it also serves as a benchmark in other respects. Although architectural investigation has become more "non-destructive," and although preservation technology has become more sophisticated, it is clearly evident that the architects had done their "homework" very well—by scouring the Tidewater countryside, photographing, sketching, and absorbing the architectural vocabulary of the 18th century building design, construction, materials, and landscape practices. This comprehensive approach was (and remains) fundamental to any restoration project—to know and understand the building at hand and its milieu. A restoration project is essentially different from ordinary construction in that it involves working *backward* from the existing building's deteriorated and altered condition to a recreation of its earlier form and appearance. Logistically, this may involve training craftsmen in long lost skills, or the replication of hand-made materials and products that are no longer available.

Peterson's report also reveals an ability, evident at the very outset of his career, to develop a wide range of contacts, especially outside the National Park Service, to assist in tracking down hitherto unrecognized old views, prints, paintings, photographs, and documents to enhance our understanding of the owners, the buildings and the landscape.

This report clearly demonstrates Peterson's ability to logistically and architecturally address a restoration project within the limitations of time and money, while maximizing the goals of conservation and accuracy within those constraints. Surely those are the challenges of all who have labored in the field of historic preservation during the intervening years since the Moore House; this report set a professional standard for all who have followed the footsteps of Charles E. Peterson in the National Park Service!

Lee H. Nelson, AIA
National Park Service
Washington, D.C., September 1981

PREFACE

During the last few years I have had the pleasure of visiting many important and interesting Early American Buildings between California, Florida, and Maine. Some of these buildings have come down to the present time more or less unchanged from their original design while others have been "done over" to suit the habits and tastes of the occupants. Quite a number have been "restored" with or without professional advice.

Curiously enough architects agree that the most interesting ancient buildings are those which have not been tampered with by other architects. In a good piece of restoration work the new parts are so skillfully blended with the old that it is difficult or impossible to separate them. The antiquarian is thus unable to give most carefully restored structures a complete and intelligent examination. The architect who planned and supervised the work had all the details in the back of his mind at the time. In a relatively few years most of the factual matter was lost or forgotten.

It is my opinion that any architect who undertakes the responsibility of working over a fine old building should feel obligated to prepare a detailed report of his findings for the information of those who will come to study it in future years. Such a volume should become a permanent part of the building—a payment by the architect for the privilege of learning and using facts which no other man may ever have. How else can we conserve the source material for the study of antique architecture?

In looking back over my five years' acquaintance with the Moore House, I have come to realize that a more or less comprehensive statement about this structure should be compiled in order that the abundant data now available will not be scattered and lost. This report is being prepared to be placed in the House so that each visitor to this historic place can know what changes have been made since it came into the hands of the Federal Government. This report is compiled from the writings, drawings, and photographs now in the possession of the National Park Service, particularly in the Branch of Plans and Design.

1

A set of drawings in the Historic American Buildings Survey, the originals of which will be found in the Library of Congress, supplement the written material.

The Introduction contains miscellaneous notes on the Moore House before 1930. The Appendixes exhibit important papers too long to be quoted in the text. Some of the material was located by the historical staff.

Several blank pages have been included at the end of each copy in order that new discoveries of important data may be noted down. I believe that a considerable body of material is yet to be found.

Charles E. Peterson
Deputy Chief Architect

October 15, 1935
Washington, D.C.

INTRODUCTION

T he Moore House is a frame farmhouse situated on the south bank of the York River a little over a mile below Yorktown, Virginia. The surrounding lands have been known for many years as "Temple Farm" and are a part of the original patent secured by John Harvey about 1631.

The date and builder of the present structure are not known. It was standing in 1781, and was owned by Augustine Moore at that time. Mr. V. M. Cruikshank of Shamokin, Pennsylvania, who was born in the Moore House, and lived there until 1895,

> ". . . stated that his father, though a Pennsylvanian, had been greatly interested in Virginia history, and was habitually a very accurate man. His father told him that the present Moore House was built in 1713."[1]

No one has been able to dispute this date though the source of the information is not known. It is quite possible, judging by Colonial houses of known date in nearby Yorktown. The Sinclair home "Thorplands", farther down the Peninsula, has some striking similarities. The excavations of 1932 revealed the remains of probably one and possibly two earlier structures within a few feet of the present house. The first graphic representations of the Moore House appear on the military maps of 1781, et seq. (Plate No. 1)

William H. Shield, owner of the Moore House from 1835 to 1840, in writing to Bishop Meade, said:

> "The house at Temple Farm is built of wood and is in rather a dilapidated condition at present. The original building was very large and consisted of a centre building with two large wings, either one of which was as large as the present house, which in fact was originally the centre building."[2]

This is a puzzling statement. A study of the existing structure in 1931, and the excavations of 1932, prove beyond a reasonable doubt that the present house was never joined by two large wings. Within the extensive area searched there were no positive evidences of detached wings. By "original building" Shield may have referred to some other structure, or his statement may simply have been an error of hearsay.

However obscure may be its history before 1781, it was an object

3

4

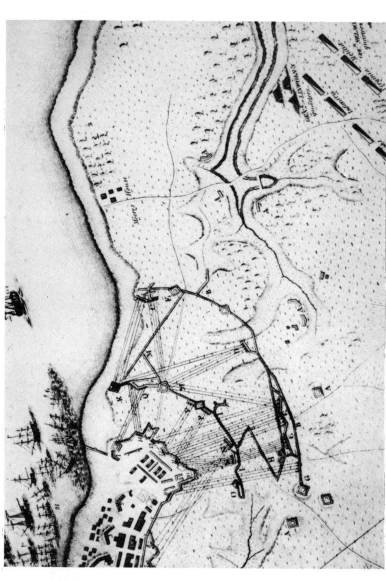

Plate No. 1: Portion of the "PLAN OF YORKTOWN IN VIRGINIA AND ADJACENT COUNTRY, Exhibiting the operations of the American, French, and English armies during the Siege of that place in October 1781. Surveyed from the 22nd to the 28th Octr. . . . . Drawn by Jn. F. Renault with a Crow-pen and presented to the MARQUIS DE LA FAYETTE." This map is one of a considerable number prepared about this time. All of them vary in details such as the number and grouping of the buildings at the Moore House. The Revolutionary maps carry the first graphic representations of the Moore House.

Plate No. 2: A photostat (enlarged) of the illustration (V 2 p. 530) in Henry Howe's "Historical Collections of Virginia," (1849). This is the earliest published view of the Moore House, brought to our attention by a loan of the volume from Mrs. A. Y. Burcher of Newport News, Virginia. This is the only information we have on the step arrangement at the rear door.

6

of interest ever after. Henry Howe published the first view in 1849 (Plate No. 2). In Lossing's "Pictorial Handbook of the Revolution" can be seen the earliest published front view known (Plate No. 3).

It is our belief that the one-story east wing (removed 1931) was built about the time of Shield's ownership. Physical evidence showed that it was an addition to the original structure and its brickwork indicated a date subsequent to 1800 (Plates Nos. 14, 15). This wing is first shown in the Civil War photographs.

Plate No. 3: A photostat (enlarged) of the illustration in Vol. II, (p. 324) Benson Lossing's "Pictorial Field Book of the Revolution," (1850). Lossing made a tour of the places associated with the Revolutionary War, visiting Yorktown in 1848. This is the second earliest known pictorial representation of the Moore House. Brought to our attention by Mr. Thomas T. Waterman, then of the Williamsburg Restoration.

Plate No. 4: Enlargement of the photograph taken by Matthew Brady in 1862, located by the writer in the Library of Congress. The decision to restore a front porch was based on a study of this photograph. There have been at least four front porches on the House, (1) an 8' by 8' porch from which the brick pier bases survive; (2) the porch shown in this photograph; (3) the porch removed in 1931 which was built probably in 1881; (4) the present porch which is a conjectural restoration of (1). This view shows the chaos of the grounds during the War which may account for the disappearance of the outbuildings. The Civil War photographs show the East Wing for the first time. This is reproduced in Miller's Photographic History of the Civil War, Vol. I, p. 269

8

Plate No. 5: The Gardner print from a negative by Wood and Gibson, May 1862. Brought to our attention by Mr. Louis R. Fiske of Upper Darby, Pennsylvania, who sold it to the writer. This view shows beyond a doubt that the building was whitewashed at the time. It also shows the interesting "swirl" of the shingles on the hips of the roof and the dormers. The size and shape of the shutter hinges is clearly indicated. Unfortunately this hitherto unknown photograph did not show up until October 8, 1931, after the roof had been reshingled according to our plans. The first opportunity to correct the effect came with the Public Works program.

The House was, fortunately, photographed twice during the Civil War—by Matthew Brady (Plate No. 4) and Wood and Gibson (the ''Gardner photograph'') (Plate No. 5). These two photographs show a remarkable amount of detail and were invaluable aids to accuracy. The text under the Gardner photograph says:

> ''When the Army of the Potomac invested Yorktown, the Moore House was in excellent preservation. It was far from a safe habitation, the rebel shells striking it several times; one in particular entered through the wall, and exploding inside, did considerable damage.''

Two excellent watercolors by McIlvaine were painted in 186–, one showing the front (Plate No. 6) and one the rear (Plate No. 7) of the building. The next picture known of the Moore House is a watercolor made by a Mr. S. H. Sankey in 1874 (Plate No. 8). The building is shown at large size as viewed from the northwest. At the time the picture was painted, apparently no appreciable change had occurred in the condition of the building since Brady's photograph was taken. The

Plate No. 6: Photograph of the McIlvaine water color painted in 186–. This painting and the one following were secured through Mr. Charles Wall, Assistant Superintendent of Mt. Vernon. They are part of a set given to President Everett of Harvard. This photograph shows a tree very similar to the gnarled old catalpa just west of the House. Just beyond is an unidentified outbuilding, possibly an ice house covering a depression in the earth which has existed for years. The desolate appearance of the building indicates (as does the Sankey water color, Plate No. 8) that the building stood in an abandoned state between the Civil War and the Centennial Celebration. Obtained through the Branch of Research and Education, Historical Division.

Plate No. 7: The second McIlvaine water color shows the rear of the House. A first glance at the original suggested red brick nogging between the framing members. Since the examination of the structure revealed no evidences of this it seems more likely to assume that it is just lath and plaster. Obtained through the Branch of Research and Education, Historical Division.

chief value of the picture is that it indicates that probably nothing in the way of improvements was done to the building between the Civil War and the 1881 rebuilding—seventeen years later. Apparently the building remained unoccupied during this time. Mr. John C. Wade of Yorktown, who worked on the building in 1881 said that it had been vandalized by negroes.

In 1881, preparatory to the Yorktown Centennial, the structure was "restored" in a typical 19th Century manner. A photograph (Plate No. 10) taken at that time, reveals the extent of the work. The freedom with which this was carried out may be surmised from a contemporary account (Appendix No. 3). Mr. Wade, who was one of the carpenters during the 1881 work, recalls that a man named Thomas Hill from Haddenfield, New Jersey, was the Foreman on the work which was done under the auspicies of the Centennial Association and was financed largely by contributions from the North. He also recalls that there were no doors, window sash, or shutters in the house when they began work there. The balustrade and some of the treads of the stairway were missing at the time and none of the old outbuildings remained.

which this was carried out may be surmised from a contemporary account (Appendix No. 3). Mr. Wade, who was one of the carpenters during the 1881 work, recalls that a man named Thomas Hill from Haddenfield, New Jersey, was the Foreman on the work which was done under the suspicies of the Centennial Association and was financed largely by contributions from the North. He also recalls that there were no doors, window sash, or shutters in the house when they began work there. The balustrade and some of the treads of the stairway were missing at the time and none of the old outbuildings remained.

The first floor of the rear wing is said to have been added at that time for the entertainment of distinguished Centennial visitors. It is believed that somewhere will be found 1881 notes which are not at present available. These may provide clues to the few details which we have had to design from our knowledge of contemporary work in other houses. The "improvements" of 1881 probably saved the house from disappearing entirely, but they give rise to some baffling questions. Why, for instance, were all of the first floor windows lowered four and one half inches?

The Centennial Association had acquired the property in connection with the 1881 celebration, but released it afterwards. From that time until 1931, the building was used as a residence. Mr. Cruikshank stated that his father had "added a considerable portion of the wings (Plate No. 16)—in 1885." This seems to have been the second story of the rear wing. A protective layer of roll roofing was added by the Williamsburg Holding Corporation which acquired the property February 26, 1929. The last tenants of the house were Mr. J. W. Shaffer and family, dairy farmers, who held a lease from the Holding Corporation.

The preceding account brings us up to the ownership by the United States and the restoration undertaken by the National Park Service. A description of the changes effected in the years 1931, 1932, 1933, and 1934, forms the body of the report following.

References
[1] Sup't. Robinson, Aug. 6, 1932, "Memorandum for File."
[2] Meade, "Old Churches, Ministers, and Families of Virginia" (1857).

Plate No. 8: Photostat of the water color painted in 1874 by Mr. S. H. Sankey. The original is owned by Mr. Thomas J. Smith, 158 East 32nd Street, New York City. This was brought to our attention through Mr. Harold Shurtleff of the Williamsburg Restoration. The accuracy of certain details is remarkable. Compare, for instance, the muntins in the northwest first floor end window with those in the Brady photograph. The southwest second floor end window may have had a total of 18 lights as suggested. The thinness of the muntins shown in the Civil War photographs may indicate that they were replacements of the original 18th Century sash.

Plate No. 9: Drawing of the Moore House from a group including views of Williamsburg. These were mounted on a small sheet of cardboard said to have been the cover of a Yorktwon Centennial program. It was loaned by Mrs. Catharine Shield. This view from the northwest shows solid panel shutters, and if these were not supplied from the artist's imagination, the sketch must have been drawn prior to the Civil War photographs. The building shown behind has not been identified. It may be the same one that appears in the Brady photograph.

14

Plate No. 10: A photostat of a photograph inlaid between pages 22 and 23 in "A History of the Monument at Yorktown, erected by the United States Government to commemorate the close of the Revolutionary War, at Yorktown, October 19, 1781", Philadelphia, 1896. This was taken probably on the occasion of the Centennial in 1881.

Plate No. 11: Photograph of the House (date unknown) some time after the Centennial, contributed to us by Mr. Walter Macomber of the Williamsburg Restoration. The cornices seem to be painted dark and it is believed that this is the olive green color found on the rear cornice when it was opened up in 1931.

16

Plate No. 11-A: Photograph copyright of 1906, reproduced from print in the Library of Congress.

Plate No. 11-B: Photograph, somewhat enlarged, of a photographic print in the possession of Mr. Peyton Nelson of Williamsburg. Kindly loaned for reproduction by the owner. The exact date of this photograph is unknown. It seems to have been taken about the same time as 11-A. (Note the stacked rifles.)

Plate No. 11-C: Photograph copyright 1911 by E. L. Owens, reproduced from print in the Library of Congress.

Plate No. 11-D: Apparently taken same day as No. 11-C (note seated figures). Reproduced from print in the Library of Congress.

Plate No. 11-E: This view seems to belong to the 1911 copyright group (note paint tones) represented in 11-C and D. Reproduced from print in the Library of Congress.

20

Plate No. 11-F: View of the interior of the "Surrender Room." Copyright 1911 by E. L. Owens. Reproduced from print in the Library of Congress.

Plate No. 12: Front view of the House, July 1931, before the 1931 restoration work. Note the Victorian window sash, shutters, door and porch. The roll roofing was a protective measure supplied by the Williamsburg Holding Corporation. The hose connection, provided by some thoughtful agency, was connected with the Navy Mine Depot water supply.

Plate No. 13: Porch detail, July 1931. This we believe to have been at least the third porch on this house. It was subsequently removed.

Plate No. 14: East wing detail, July 1931. This wing is thought to have been added somewhere between 1800 and the Civil War. Its foundations are of common bond, whereas those of the main structure are of Flemish.

Plate No. 15: Details of East and Rear Wings, July 1931. Certain doorways had to be cut in the original framing of the house to allow access to the wings.

No 1596

Plate No. 16: Rear View, July 1931. The rear wing was built at two different times: the lower floor was added for ''the entertainment of distinguished visitors'' in 1881, and the upper floor by John Cruikshank about 1886. A third dormer was torn away during the Cruikshank additions, but part of the framing remained in the walls.

Plate No. 17: Southwest corner detail, July 1931. The rear cornice was largely buried under the Victorian porch roof. Original modillion blocks, when removed were found to be of poplar fixed in place with wrought nails.

26

Plate No. 18: Northwest corner detail, July 1931. The tin flashing, patchy mortar and whitewash were subsequently removed from the brickwork.

Plate No. 19: Largest of the outbuildings found on the property. Demolished just after photograph was taken in July 1931.

28

Plate No. 20: More outbuildings, July 1931. One not shown in these plates was a double maple bowling alley in the orchard.

Plate No. 21: Central hall, July 1931. Note modern door and lighting fixture. Both were removed in 1931 and 1932.

Plate No. 22: Main stairway, July 1931. The typical 19th Century balustrade was removed in 1933–34.

Plate No. 23: Door to cellar stairs, July 1931. The stairway had been cut through early floor joists showing that this space had been a closet originally. The room beyond seems to have been a closet for some time. Its partition walls are of uncertain date.

31

Plate No. 24: Stairway detail, July 1931. The left branch of the stairway was found to be of modern construction cut through old joists and was removed and sealed up in 1932.

Plate No. 25: Stairway detail, July 1931. The modern stringer, rail, and balusters continued across the wall. They were thought to have been 1881 construction.

Plate No. 26: East Room view, July 1931. The mantel was obviously Victorian and replaced in 1932. The corner door led into the East wing. The cornice was replaced by one of simple Colonial design in 1933–4. On the back of one of the first floor mantels was found the pencil notation "Col. Peyton, Yorktown." This man was probably an officer in charge during the 1881 work.

Plate No. 27: East Room view, July 1931. The interior doors throughout the house with their Victorian panels, mortise locks, and china knobs were replaced in 1932.

34

Plate No. 28: First floor room in the East wing, July 1931. Just before the removal of the entire wing.

Plate No. 29: The ''Surrender Room'' fireplace, July 1931. The double door on the left was replaced by a single door in 1932 in accordance with the evidence in the framing and local precedent.

36

Plate No. 30: The "Surrender Room" in July 1931. The use of this room in Colonial times is not known. The writer suspects that the Committee of officers preparing the terms would have looked for a dining room table.

Plate No. 31: The room behind the "Surrender Room", July 1931. The interior door and window trim throughout the house are typical 18th Century in design and it is not known how much was replaced and added in 1881.

Plate No. 32: Room behind the "Surrender Room" July 1931. The chair rail shown in the picture ran throughout the three principal rooms of the first floor. The chair rail found in the building was not a typical Colonial detail and its age is uncertain.

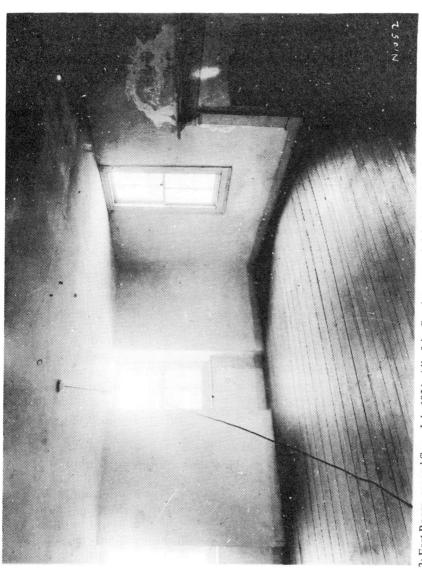

Plate No. 33: East Room, second floor, July 1931. All of the fireplaces were bricked up when the United States acquired the House. When the openings were cleared of the brick, detailed drawings were made of each condition in order to better approximate the proper size and shape of each.

Plate No. 34: Northwest room, second floor, 1931. This room shares the end chimney with the room behind. Diagonal fireplaces like this are a common arrangement in early Virginia buildings.

Plate No. 35: Southwest room, second floor, July 1931. While much of the original flooring remained in the building, it was patched with modern boards in many places. Antique flooring was used to correct the effect during the 1933–4 work.

42

Plate No. 36: View looking east in the cellar. July, 1931. The stair shown on the right was modern and has been removed. Access was originally had through an outside entrance which has been restored.

Plate No. 37: West chimney foundation, July 1935. The brick partitions on the left were modern and were removed after the first floor framing was repaired.

44

Plate No. 38: Remains of the original cellar entrance, July, 1931. On the right side can be seen the broken surfaces where the sidewall was torn away. On the left the wall had been largely rebuilt to meet new conditions in the rear wing. The oak nosing of the lowest brick step was sunk into the square holes to be seen on either side.

45

Plate No. 39: Detail of framing, southeast corner of the first floor, July 1931. The corner post and cross-brace were badly rotted and had been patched.

Plate No. 40: Framing detail, July 1931. When some of the weatherboarding was removed it was discovered that the tenons of the framing of the first floor windows had been cut and the frames dropped between four and five inches. We do not know the reason for this.

Plate No. 41: Roof framing detail, July 1931. The Roman numerals on the poplar rafters were marked there to assist the carpenters in assembling the framework of the house.

THE RESTORATION WORK OF 1931

On December 29, 1930, in a letter to Director Horace M. Albright, Congressman S. O. Bland of Virginia proposed that the Moore House and surrounding land be purchased as a part of the preparations for the Yorktown Sesquicentennial celebration of 1931.[1] The Federal Government was enabled to do this by the Act of Congress of July 3, 1930, creating the Colonial National Monument. This idea was received with favor and negotiations with the Williamsburg Holding Corporation were immediately begun.

At this time the Moore House was in run-down condition and presented a wholly different picture than it did in 1781. The house had been more than doubled in size by incongruous additions. The roof looked bad and the Victorian window sash, doors, and blinds affected the design and scale of the whole. The main building was surrounded by a motley group of shacks, including even an indoor bowling alley. In view of the approaching Sesquicentennial with a multitude of visitors expected, the writer felt it advisable to recommend that some rehabilitation be attempted. The project was initiated in a memorandum to the Director dated November 27, 1930.[2]

In the appropriation for developing the Colonial National Monument there were no funds available for restoration and it was some time before a method of financing could be worked out. It was finally proposed that the purchase price be extended to cover the work desired, and on May 23 Director Albright wired Mr. Chorley of the Holding Corporation:

". . . Moore House acquisition in status that permits reasonable restoration by you and funds of approximately eight thousand available for increase in price to cover work to be done Stop Wish you would consider new roof, Colonial windows, painting and removal modern additions Stop Peterson has details."

A procedure was worked out whereby work might proceed during and after the transfer of the property. The Moore House and the surrounding grounds were transferred to the United States on July 1, 1931, for a consideration of $46,051.28.

On May 7, Messrs. J. R. Thrower and W. M. Haussmann of the Landscape Division (now the Branch of Plans and Design) began the measuring of the building. A very detailed set of measured drawings was eventually completed.[3] Drawings for estimating the proposed work were also prepared.[4] The drawings call for the removal of the East and rear wings, the installation of new exterior doors, window sash, and basement grilles, the substitution of a small stoop for the long rear porch, a replacement of the existing front porch, the rebuilding of the cellar bulkhead, and complete reroofing. The nature of these drawings is explained in a memorandum from the writer to Engineer-in-Charge Taylor, June 26:

> "The drawings show, as far as is possible without any excavation or inspection of the interior frame work, what will, with the moderate sum available, bring back some of the Colonial flavor that the building had in 1781. It was realized that this work cannot be called a restoration of the house; it is only an attempt to correct the more obvious post-Colonial mutations in an effort to improve the appearance of this building for the Sesquicentennial Celebration."

These drawings were transmitted to the Holding Corporation June 27, for an estimate by Todd and Brown contractors for the Williamsburg Restoration.

On July 6, two carpenters from the Restoration reported and an examination of the framing began. Several features were found:

1. The sills were of hewn oak and in such good condition as to indicate their placement in 1881. The framing immediately above, probably the original, was in bad condition (Plate No. 39). The roof framing of poplar, mortised and pegged with the usual marking in Roman numerals, was in excellent condition (Plate No. 41).

2. The original cornice under the rear porch roof. Some of the poplar modillions had been replaced.

3. That all first floor windows had been lowered four and a half inches from their original mortised location (Plate No. 40).

4. The third rear dormer framing buried in a closet wall. The location checks with that shown in the rear view in Howe.

5. The remains of the original cellar bulkhead entrance under the East wing (Plate No. 38).

6. The exterior chimney enclosed by the East wing was in fairly complete condition except that like the other, it had been painted and clumsily flashed. Rain had leaked in at several points.

7. A rear first floor window had been cut down to allow a doorway to the pantry in the rear wing.

8. The upper left wing of the main stairway had been cut through the original joists to give access to the second floor of the rear wing (Plate No. 24).

9. The three second floor end windows which remained seem to be in their original locations.

Excavations began on July 10 and additional facts were ascertained:

1. Shallow sinkings in the side walls of the cellar entrance formerly receiving the oak nosing of brick steps indicated the position and dimension of the three bottom steps.

2. No remains or indications of any cellar flooring were found.

3. No remains of any rear steps were found. However, certain brick walls unrelated to the house under restoration were uncovered. (These were completely uncovered in 1932—see Appendix No. 10.)

4. Four piers 17″ by 17″ of Colonial brick, same size as those in the original house, were found in the ground in front of the river on front entrance. These indicated the existence of an early porch of smaller dimension than and superceding the porch shown on the photographs of 1862. The original stumps of these piers, about three courses high, still remain in the ground.

The above discoveries enabled us to complete our detailed plans. These were checked and approved by Perry, Shaw, and Hepburn, the architects of the Williamsburg Restoration. Notice to proceed with the work was given August 15 in a letter from Mr. Taylor to Mr. V. M. Geddy of the Holding Corporation:

". . . It is satisfactory for you to proceed with the work in accord with your letter of August 13th, with the understanding that if there is a balance remaining after this work is completed that this balance will be used for additional work which has previously been listed or which will later be designated."

Workmen started demolishing the wings on August 20 and the new construction started shortly afterwards. Mr. Paul Houck represented Todd and Brown on the ground, and Mr. Thrower the Landscape Division.

The work proceeded as expeditiously as possible with the Sesquicentennial opening as a deadline. It was learned early in October that there would be a surplus of funds and that a limited number of additional items might be undertaken. Accordingly Todd and Brown were requested to provide panelled wood shutters and new shutter fasteners, to open the bricked-up fireplaces, and to install a number of small miscellaneous items. The plastering was patched and painted, and the "Surrender Room" was outfitted with a hastily assembled group of antique furnishings (Plate No. 47). The building was opened to the public on Friday, October 16. In its incomplete state the building probably looked very much the way it did in 1781. At the same time, however, the cellar was full of props supporting the girders and joists weakened by rot and insects. The interior still had its Victorian doors and mantels, but the deadline had been met.

In the rear of the Moore House and symmetrical to it, two small frame comfort stations were erected under contract with Allen J. Saville. The new Yorktown water system was extended to the Moore House for fire protection furnished by two hydrants on either side of the building, built into the ground to make them inconspicuous. The electric and telephone services to the House were placed underground.

References

[1] Appendix No. 4.
[2] Appendix No. 5.
[3] Branch of Plans and Design file COL-1031. These have been retraced and form Historic American Buildings Survey Project No. VA-80 in the Library of Congress.
[4] COL-1031-A (in part).

Plate No. 42: The first reconstruction program rushing towards completion for the Sesquicentennial, early autumn 1931.

54

Plate No. 43: Rear view of the House, early autumn, 1931. The third dormer has just been put back and handsplit cypress shingles from Charleston, S.C., put down.

55

Plate No. 44: Front view of the house as put in shape for the Sesquicentennial Celebration, October 1931. The shutters are adopted from those formerly on the house of Miss Annie Galt of Williamsburg. The size of the window lights and the details of the sash are typical of the period in Tidewater Virginia.

Plate No. 45: View of southeast corner after restoration work of 1931. Shortage of funds and time did not enable us to raise the window frames or complete the cleaning down of the chimney brick.

57

Plate No. 46: View of southwest corner after restoration work of 1931. The rear stoop was a conjectural design similar to those used in Williamsburg. The discovery of the illustration in Howe suggested the simpler arrangement which replaced this one in 1933–4.

58

Plate No. 47: The "Surrender Room" as furnished and exhibited by Superintendent Robinson during the Sesquicentennial Celebration.

THE EXCAVATIONS OF 1932

While the Moore House itself had come down to us in fairly good condition, none of the outbuildings so typical of the early Virginia plantation had survived the two hundred years. It was our plan to eventually restore the grounds as of 1781, thus providing a proper background for the house. No helpful clue regarding the location of Colonial outbuildings is afforded by the military maps of 1781, though many of them indicate that such buildings existed. With more funds available there was set up in the budget an item for exploratory excavations. It seemed almost inevitable that remains of additional buildings would be uncovered. Ordinarily the foundation footings are left after the remainder of the building is destroyed.

Work was begun about February 1 under the direction of Mr. Haussmann with David P. Smith as foreman. The ground was trenched in a gridiron pattern on ten foot centers. A depression about fifty feet southeast of the present house yielded a small but interesting foundation of marlstone and brick (Plate No. 54). This structure was designated as Building No. 1. What the building was originally can only be surmised. It may have been an outbuilding. The fireplace, of which part of the sides and hearth remained, seemed to indicate living quarters since it was much smaller than those usually found in outside kitchens. The building may or may not have had a marlstone superstructure. Grace Church in Yorktown is the only building of this type that has. It has been suggested that this was the earliest residence on the Temple Farm and was succeeded by two others of which the present structure is the later. The earliest known reference to buildings on this land is a title conveyance of 1686.

The remains of a structure approximately equal in size and shape to the present building were found just behind and not quite parallel to it (Plate No. 48). This was designated as Building No. 2. The foundations are of brick and marl, unusual in outline. Apparently the superstructure was of wood and there was no basement. In one corner there is a hollow rectangle of brick 5'5" by 7'10" of unknown use. It is believed that these fragments remain from a house of very early date since it is too close to the present structure to have stood at the same time. The character of the objects found seems to be very early—particularly the parts of the small brass clock. The writer recalls seeing a similar clock with brass filigree work in a 17th Century American room in the Metropolitan Museum of Art.

Civil War photographs show that the grounds about the house were extensively torn up and it is likely that any outbuildings remaining were razed and the parts used for hasty military constructions. There are in the ground a number of depressions filled with rubbish which may mark the sites of disappeared buildings. Probably what saved the foundations of Buildings Nos. 1 and 2 was the fact that they were not in view at the time of the War.

Nearly four hundred dollars were spent on this exploratory work which was concluded in May. The foundations of Building No. 1 were left exposed for a time and then removed during the construction of the heating plant in 1934. The foundations of Building No. 2 were covered with earth and marked on the surface with dry-laid brick. For additional information refer to Appendix No. 7, and the drawings of the Historic American Buildings Survey.

The circular depression under the catalpa tree southwest of the house yielded practically nothing. Its history goes back at least to the time when Mr. Cruikshank lived there. He remembered it to be in practically the same condition. An ice house with pit walls of log cribbing may have occupied the site. The marl lined well in front of the house is thought to be very old. The investigation did not disclose any new information about it.

The results of the exploration were in general disappointing and the location of any reconstructed outbuildings will have to be conjectural.

Plate No. 48: Photograph of the excavation of ''Building No. 2'', 1932. The foundation is a shallow one of marl and brick and is thought to be the remains of a house earlier than the present structure (see Appendix).

THE RESTORATION WORK OF 1932

W hen it was discovered that a total of $2,353.95 was still available from the original allotment, it was decided that every effort should be made to rebuild the interior as authentically as possible and to pursue certain lines of documentary research which had hitherto been impossible through lack of funds. The Holding Corporation agreed to act as disbursing agent, the Park Service employing the laborers and executing the work according to the plans of the Landscape Division.

"It is to be regretted that interior work must be done before the replacement of major structural parts in the framing is effected. However . . . the building must be opened as a public exhibit . . ."[1]

It was finally decided to repair the fireplaces and chimneys, replace the mantels and interior doors with Colonial types, and to close off the left hand wing of the stairway. On April 27, 1932, a laborer began the removal of plaster from the chimney breasts. It was apparent that most of the brickwork around the fireplaces had been removed and replaced— some with old brick and some with modern. Careful study was made of existing conditions and highly detailed drawings made. These can be seen in the Historic American Buildings Survey.

The framing of the double door leading from the "Surrender Room" to the rear room was investigated and it was found that a door of typical size, probably the original, had once existed there. This opening was reframed and new doors hung throughout the house, replacing those apparently installed in 1881. The doors in the interesting house of Mrs. Conway Shield of Yorktown were studied for precedent.

The partitions in the rear of the left front room were examined, but because of conflicting evidence it was decided to leave them where they were. There is some question as to their age. They may not have been built with the house originally, but added before 1781. (The accepted policy for the development of Yorktown is to bring back conditions as they were in the summer of 1781 while the town was occupied by the British before destructive firing began.) The floor plan in that part of the house is peculiar, but not at all impossible. The plastering was again patched and repainted in the existing colors. The morning of July 1, the work was completed in accordance with the request of the Director and turned over to the Superintendent. A complete account of the 1932 work may be found in Appendix No. 8.

At this time a small amount of money was spent in minor improvements to the grounds and certain plantings, including the clematis vine on the front porch. A number of pieces of antique furniture were purchased for furnishing the "Surrender Room," though the funds available were not sufficient to complete the effect.

References
[1] Charles E. Peterson, letter to the Director, January 5, 1932.

Plate No. 49: Beginning of the Public Works program October, 1933. The dormers were removed for rebuilding and the framing shored up for the removal of the first floor joists.

THE RESTORATION WORK OF 1933–34

The Yorktown Sesquicentennial Association had a surplus of funds on deposit with the American Bank and Trust Company of Richmond. At a meeting of the Board of Trustees at Yorktown on November 14, 1932, a resolution was adopted appropriating $2500 for the restoration and preservation of some of the ancient York County records.

"The balance of the fund was appropriated to the restoration of the Moore House, subject to the holding of one thousand dollars for twelve months with which to meet current obligations. The following Committee was appointed to supervise the restoration of the Moore House:

A. J. Renforth, Yorktown
George P. Coleman, Williamsburg
Kenneth Chorley, Williamsburg
Mrs. E. E. Holland, Suffolk
A representative of the National Park Service, to be appointed by the Director.
Oliver J. Sands, Richmond
Wm. A. R. Goodwin, Williamsburg.

A resolution was passed directing that the funds of the Y.S.A. be turned over to the Committee appointed for the restoration of the Moore House, to be expended by them in accordance with the resolutions of the Trustees. Of this Committee, Mr. Oliver J. Sands, of Richmond, was elected Treasurer."[1]

Superintendent Robinson was appointed as a member of this committee by the Director of the National Park Service.

The Sesquicentennial Association and the National Park Service accepted the offer of Perry, Shaw, and Hepburn, Williamsburg Restoration architects, to donate plans for completing the restoration work. The study and drawings were principally by Messrs. William Perry, Walter Macomber, Clyde Trudell and Foster Townsend of that organization. All of the drawings and data gathered by the Landscape Division were turned over to these architects and one or two conferences were held with the writer which enabled the architects to utilize all of the information then available.

The Restoration Committee voted to approve the plans at a meeting September 25, 1933. At that time, however, the funds of the Association had been impounded through the failure of the bank. In the meantime the

67

U.S. Public Works Administration had approved a construction program for the National Park Service and an allotment of $22,500 was made available for the restoration of the Moore House, and a detached building for heating purposes. (Federal Project No. 222.)

Assistant Architect Clyde F. Trudell, who had in the meantime become associated with the Branch of Plans and Design, was designated as architectural inspector and Mr. Hurst, recently of Todd and Brown, was appointed foreman. Work was begun in October 1933.

During this work program concrete footings were placed under the foundation walls, modern brick cellar partitions removed, defective sills, girders, joists and bracing replaced on the first and second floors, and the main stair rail and balusters replaced by an 18th Century design. The interior basement stairway was removed, a Colonial type door put in to replace the one found there and the space made into a closet. The key block of the first floor east room mantel was slightly changed. All of the plaster had been removed during the investigation of the house. This was replaced and the interiors painted in various colors in accordance with Georgian precedent. The rear stoop was replaced by the simple tread and stringer arrangement indicated in Howe's illustration. A brick gutter was run around the outside of the house. The shutters installed in 1931 were replaced by solid panel shutters of slightly different design as indicated in Plate No. 9. The roof was insulated and reshingled after the interesting manner shown so clearly in the "Gardner" photograph (unknown when the building was shingled in 1931).

All of the first floor windows were raised to their original positions. The fifteen light window sash (1931) of the front dormers were changed to twelve light sash because of the sash remains to be noted in the Gardner photograph. The muntins of the Civil War period appear to be very thin and it hardly seems likely that they were in the original sash. The fifteen light sash (1931) were retained in the rear dormers because they are more typical of the period. The Sankey water color would indicate that the second floor end windows had eighteen light sash. The dormers might also have had them. Further evidence is needed here.

Methods for heating the building received a great deal of discussion. In order to retain the wood shingles it was decided to locate the boiler outside of the main building in a restoration of Building No. 1. A heating plant with the exterior a conjectural reconstruction of the original building was designed and built. The layout carries underground pipes to the main building and radiation is effected by concealed units.

All work was completed in September and the building dedicated on October 18, 1934, by the Director of the National Park Service, Arno B. Cammerer.

NOTE ON THE LANDSCAPE WORK

At a meeting of the Sesquicentennial Association's Committee for the restoration of the Moore House, December 14, 1933, it was voted to accept the kind offer of Mr. Arthur A. Schurcliff to prepare plans for the development of the Moore House grounds. Mr. Shurcliff is Landscape Architect of the Williamsburg Restoration and has done a great deal of research on the layouts and plant materials of early Virginia plantations.

General plans were prepared by Mr. Shurcliff and approved by the National Park Service. These plans are being carried out at the present time by Civilian Conservation Corps workers.

References
[1] Report by Dr. Wm. A. R. Goodwin, Nov. 23, 1932.

Plate No. 50: Rear view of the house during 1933–4 work. The first floor windows have been raised and the second floor windows resashed. A typical double ogee moulding was run all around the building where the roof plane breaks.

Plate No. 51: Framing detail, southwest first floor room, 1933. All the plaster in the building was removed at this time.

Plate No. 52: Stairway framing, 1933. Mortise hole of one of the joists originally supporting the closet floor under the stairs can be seen. The closet, including a new door, was restored in 1933–4.

73

Plate No. 53: Upstairs framing, 1933, showing shingle nailing strips and the furring of the walls.

Plate No. 54: The remains of the building east of the main house measured 22′-4½″ by 22′-7″. For the most part they are of local marl. The fireplace lining and hearth were of typical handmade brick. The identity of this building is unknown. It was reconstructed as an outbuilding to the present house to hold the heating plant. These foundations were removed at that time.

Plate No. 55: Shingling the roof of the heating building, 1934.

Appendices

APPENDIX NO. 1

"Temple Farm—Ludlow Patent

"To all &c Whereas &c Now Know yee That I ye said Richard Bennet Esqr &c Give and Grant unto Coll Geo Ludlow Esqr one of ye Councel of State for this Colony fifteen hundred acres of land scituate, lying and being in ye County of York, beginning att ye mouth of a Creek on ye south side of Charles River called Wormelays Creek and from thence running up ye river five hundred eighty three po: unto certaine marked trees, and from thence runneth south west into ye woods alongst certaine mark'd trees three hundred and twenty po: then south East twenty fouer po: to a certaine mark'd ash tree thence South west two hundred and twenty po: to a swamp called ye Green Swamp alonge certaine mark'd trees dividing ye land of Capt: Nicholas Marteau and ye said Coll George Ludlow and from ye said swamp one hundred po: south west by south, then south one hundred and fouerteen po: adjoining to ye mill land belonging to Warwick river from thence north East three hundred and ninety five po: thence south East three hundred po: and thence south west from thence three hundred and twenty po: *wh* three lines are bounded in Hugh Allends land, thence south East three hundred and twenty po: then north north East halfe a point Easterly from a run of water that runs into ye small new Poquoson three hundred and twenty po: ane then north East parrallel to ye land late Capt Wormeleys; The said land being due unto ye said Coll George Ludlow Esqr as followeth viz fouerteen hundred fifty two acres part hereof being formerly granted unto him by Pattent dated ye twenty sixth of July 1646 and due unto him as in ye said Pattent is att large mentioned in ye records and forty eight acres ye residue by order of ye Governor and Councell dated ye twentieth of March 1652 and also by and for ye transportation of one person &c To have and to hold &c yielding and Paying &c W*ch* payment is to be made &c Dated ye twenty sixth of March 1652

Patents 3, 23—Land Office
State Capitol, Richmond, Virginia"

APPENDIX NO. 2

"Chain of Title To The Moore House

"1. John Wiles and wife, Elizabeth, and Peter Temple and wife, Mary, conveyed the tract including site of the Moore House to Lawrence Smith on November 6, 1686 by warranty deed.
D.O.W. #7, p. 270.

"2. Lawrence Smith, the elder, deviced this tract to his son, Lawrence Smith, by will bearing date of August 8, 1700. Smith senior died about the year 1700. This will is not recorded but the above facts in regard to it appear from an ejection suit brought by Robert Westlake against Lawrence Smith, Jr., in which Smith's title was confirmed by the court.
O.W. #15, last page (not numbered)

"3. By will probated March 19, 1738, Lawrence Smith left the Temple Farm to his wife, Mildred, for life, remainder to his son, Robert Smith.
W&I #18, p. 487.

"4. The life estate in Mildred Smith was terminated in 1754 and title passed to her son, Robert, under his father's will.

"5. On April 30, 1767, Robert Smith mortgaged the Temple Farm to Hon. William Nelson to secure a debt due to Nelson.
Deeds #VII, p. 312.

"6. On July 6, 1767, Robert Smith placed a second mortgage on the farm in favor of David Jameson.
Deeds VII, p. 357.

"7. On August 14, 1768, Robert Smith and wife, Mary, conveyed the Temple Farm to Augustine Moore by warranty deed.
Deeds VII, p. 440.

"8. On December 18, 1769, Hon. William Nelson conveyed his mortgage to Augustine Moore for valuable consideration.
Deeds VIII, p. 29.

"9. On the same date, David Jameson, conveyed his second mortgage to Augustine Moore for value.
Deeds #VIII, p. 29.

"10. By will probated September 15, 1788, Augustine Moore

devised a life estate in the Temple Farm to his wife, Lucy, with remainder to General Thomas Nelson.
W&I #23, p. 164.

"11. By will probated February 16, 1789, General Thomas Nelson devised his remainder to the Moore property to his son, Hugh Nelson.
W&I #23, p. 171.

"12. The life estate of Mrs. Lucy Moore was terminated by her death in October, 1797.

"13. On May 22, 1818, Hugh Nelson conveyed by warranty deed the Moore property to Thomasia, Thomas and George W. Nelson.
D.B. #8, p. 507.

"14. On May 8, 1821, Thomas Nelson, George W. Nelson, Carter Berkley and Francis N., his wife, and William Meade and Thomasia, his wife, conveyed the Moore property to John Baily.
D.B. #9, p. 92.

"15. On August 26, 1824, John Baily conveyed by warranty deed to Matthew Guy.
D.B. #9, p. 450.

"16. On January 2, 1830, Baily gave another deed to Guy to correct defects in the previous one.
D.B. #11, p. 87.

"17. On February 27, 1830, Matthew Guy conveyed by warranty deed to Thomas Newman.
D.B. #11, p. 106.

"18. On January 1, 1835, Thomas Newman and Susan M., his wife, conveyed to Wm. H. Shield by warranty deed.
D.B. #12, p. 26.

"19. On January 1, 1840, William Henry Shield and Anna Byrd, his wife, conveyed by warranty deed to William M. Pettitt.
D.B. #13, p. 542.

"20. On January 1, 1854, William M. Pettitt and Louisa W., his wife, conveyed by warranty deed to James P. Silby.
D.B. #16, p. 39.

"21. On same date James P. Silby conveyed to James W. Curtis, trustee, to secure the payment of the purchase price.
D.B. #16, p. 41.

"22. On December 10, 1857, James P. Silby and Willimina, his wife, and James W. Curtis, trustee, under the deed of trust and Wm. M. Pettitt, beneficiary under the deed of trust conveyed with general warranty to Samuel C. White.
D.B. #16, p. 261.

"23. On same date Samuel C. White conveyed to William S. Peachy, trustee, to secure the payment of the purchase price.
D.B. #16, p. 263.

"24. On April 12, 1866, Samual C. White and Mary N., his wife, conveyed to Nathaniel F. Williams, trustee, to secure the payment of certain debts set out in the deed of trust.
D.B. #16, p. 599.

"25. On July 23, 1869, after default Nathaniel F. Williams conveyed to Clara M. Hewson, all the right, title and interest that Samuel C. White then had in the property.
D.B. #17, p. 231.

"26. On February 28, 1870, Clara M. Hewson conveyed to William D. Shurtz.
D.B. #17, p. 293.

"27. On same date William D. Shurtz conveyed to Nathaniel F. Williams, trustee, to secure the payment of the purchase price. This was released by Williams, Trustee by deed, dated April 16, 1881.
D.B. #17, p. 294.

"28. On December 22, 1873, William D. Shurtz conveyed to Walter B. Brooks, trustee, all his property to secure his creditors.
D.B. #18, p. 431.

"29. On March 29, 1881, William S. Peachy, trustee, released his interest to William D. Shurtz.
D.B. #19, p. 491.

"30. On April 12, 1881, Walter B. Brooks, Trustee, released his interest to William D. Shurtz.
D.B. #19, p. 503.

"31. On May 5, 1881, William D. Shurtz and wife conveyed to the Yorktown Centennial Association with general warranty.
D.B. #19, p. 504.

"32. On May 23, 1881, the Yorktown Centennial Association

conveyed to Rubin Foster, trustee, to secure a debt.
D.B. #19, p. 535.

"33. In 1882 Neeley and Company filed a Mechanics Lien for lumber and supplies furnished the Yorktown Centennial Association. Judgment Docket, p. 58.

"34. In 1882 Neeley and Company filed suit in Chancery Court to subject the Temple Farm to their judgment. The land was sold to B. W. Ford.
File #17.

"35. On July 6, 1883, B. W. Ford conveyed Temple Farm to A. J. Ford, trustee, to secure a debt set forth in the deed. This deed of trust was released April 27, 1886.
D.B. #20, p. 26; Released D.B. #1, p. 12.

"36. On April 27, 1886, B. W. Ford conveyed Temple Farm with general warranty to John Cruikshank.
D.B. #21, p. 27.

"37. On same date Cruikshank conveyed Temple Farm to A. J. Ford, trustee to secure the payment of the purchase price. This deed of trust was released to Cruikshank, May 23, 1891.
D.B. #21, p. 28; Release D.B. #1, p. 53.

"38. On May 20, 1891, John Cruikshank and wife conveyed to Thomas Tabb, trustee, to secure a debt set forth in the deed. This deed of trust was released to Cruikshank December 28, 1895.
D.B. #22, p. 194; Release D.B. #1, p. 95.

"39. On August 10, 1895, John Cruikshank and wife conveyed Temple Farm with general warranty to Amos O. Mauch.
D.B. #23, p. 290.

"40. On same date Amos O. Mauch and wife conveyed to N. L. Henley and Thomas Tabb, trustee, to secure the purchase price. This was released in part on January 3, 1911 and entirely on March 3, 1911.
D.B. #23, p. 291.

"41. On September 14, 1900, Amos O. Mauch and wife conveyed, subject to the former trust to Alexander McIntosh, trustee, to secure a debt set out in the deed. This was released June 20, 1905.
D.B. #25, p. 104; Release D.B. #1, p. 215.

"42. On June 20, 1905 Amos O. Mauch and wife conveyed to R.

T. Armistead, trustee, subject to the Cruikshank deed of trust. This was released June 28, 1910.
D.B. #27, p. 374.

"43. On June 10, 1905, Amos O. Mauch and wife conveyed to Joseph W. Mauck with general warranty but subject to above encumbrances.
D.B. #27, p. 371.

"44. Soon afterwards (date unknown) Joseph W. Mauch, and wife executed to Amos O. Mauck their power of attorney to rent, sell, lease, etc.

"45. On August 21, 1905, acting under the power of attorney Amos O. Mauck contracted to sell to R. T. Armistead. This was barred by the Statute of Limitations.
D.B. #27, p. 404.

"46. On August 21, 1905 by Amos O. Mauch conveyed with general warranty to William R. Iaeger.
D.B. #27, p. 514.

"47. On December 14, 1910, William R. Iaeger and wife conveyed to John Wymouth, trustee, to secure a debt.
D.B. #31, p. 87.

"48. On April 3, 1914, the deed of trust to Wymouth was released.
D.B. #31, p. 87.

"49. On March 28, 1914 William R. Iaeger and wife conveyed to Carter Bowie and Frank Armistead, trustees, to secure payment of a debt. This was released February 13, 1918.
D.B. #33, p. 340.

"50. On October 6, 1919, William R. Iaeger conveyed with general warranty to his wife, Martha C. Iaeger, that portion of the Temple Farm, including the Moore House, which he still owned.
D.B. #25A, p. 427.

"51. On October 8, 1919, Martha C. Iaeger, appointed William R. Iaeger, her true and lawful attorney.
D.B. #36, p. 496.

"Since this date the property has been subdivided and the title has passed through various hands.

Charles S. Marshall

October 5, 1935"   By _____ Junior Historian _____

APPENDIX NO. 3

"The following are extracts from a printed prospectus of the 1881 Yorktown celebration, dated September 1, 1881, issued from the office of the Secretary of the Yorktown Centennial Association, the Exchange Hotel, Richmond:

PROGRAMME

Thursday, October 13.—The formal opening of the Moore House (the scene of the Capitulation) and the inauguration of the Celebration by an address from the President of the Association with a reunion of the descendants of officers and soldiers of the Revolution.

THE CAMP-GROUND—

—is upon the Temple Farm, purchased by the Yorktown Centennial Association for the purpose, and which has been laid out under the direction of Lieutenant-Colonel William P. Craighill and corps of engineers. The farm is between 400 and 500 acres in extent, a level platform at an elevation of from 50 to 70 feet above the water line, and with a frontage of about 1-½ miles on the York River, commanding an unobstructed view of the extensive surrounding waters of the river (two miles wide) and the Chesapeake Bay. A more suitable spot for a military and naval display combined could not be found anywhere, and during the Celebration will present a scene of unparalleled beauty and animation. The soil is of that sandy composition, draining itself almost immediately after the heaviest rains.

"MOORE'S HOUSE, the scene of capitulation, an object of much interest, still standing upon the farm, has been restored and put in thorough repair (observing the original model—the same floors, doors and window frames, fireplaces, &c., remaining undisturbed) for the reception of distinguished guests, and will be open to free access by all visitors to the Celebration. The house will be furnished throughout in the most gorgeous style by contributions from prominent carpet, furniture and paper hangings manufacturers of the country, bronzes and bric-a-brac, from Messrs. Tiffany & Co., of New York. In the room where the terms of surrender were prepared, a handsomely bound register, presented to the Association by Mr. Mann of Philadelphia, will be placed for the registration of the autographs of visitors. In this room also, revolutionary relics will be placed upon exhibition, for the safekeeping of which the Association pledge their responsibility.

"A MAMMOTH PAVILION will be erected upon the grounds by the Association in close proximity to Moore's House, to be used for restaurant purposes throughout the day, for grand balls in the evening, possibly for sleeping quarters, and for the holding of divine services on Sunday, the 16th."

APPENDIX NO. 4.

"The United States
Yorktown Sesquicentennial Commission
Washington

December 29, 1930.

"Mr. Horace N. Albright,
Director of National Park Service,
Washington, D. C.

Dear Mr. Albright:

"At a meeting of the United States Yorktown Sesquicentennial Commission, held on the 18th day of December, 1930, Dr. W. A. R. Goodwin, of Williamsburg, Va., appeared before the Commission, and brought to the attention of the Commission that a few years past, when a hearing was held before the Committee of the Library of the House of Representatives on a bill for the creation of the Yorktown Sesquicentennial Commission and on a bill for the purchase of the Moore House at Yorktown, Virginia, in which the terms of the surrender were negotiated, it was represented by members of the Committee on the Library that if the Moore House should be bought by private interests and taken off the market where it was in danger of being bought by speculators, efforts would be made to have the United States acquire said Moore House as a part of the Sesquicentennial celebration, though it was understood that no definite commitments were or could be made.

"Dr. Goodwin stated that the property had been bought by Mr. John D. Rockefeller, Jr., at the cost approximately of $30,000.00 and that the United States could now buy the said property at the price paid by Mr. Rockefeller and without interest and taxes.

"Dr. Goodwin called attention to the absence of any item for the purchase in the budget of the Commission, and urged that it be included. It was the sense of the Commission, however, that as provision had been made by law for the establishment of the Colonial National Monument in the State of Virginia to include parts of the battlefield at Yorktown and historic points there, and as the Moore House should be acquired as a part of said monument, the purchase should be made by the National Park Service out of appropriations to be made for the Colonial National Monument.

"The Secretary of the Commission was directed to bring the situation to the attention of the National Park Service, and pursuant to said direction, I am bringing this matter to your attention with the hope that the National Park Service will acquire this property from Mr. Rockefeller at the price paid by him for the property.

"Yours very sincerely,

(Sgd.) S. O. Bland,

Secretary, U. S. Yorktown
Sesquicentennial Commission.''

APPENDIX NO. 5.

"Williamsburg, Virginia

"November 27, 1930.

"Memorandum to the Director:

"The Moore House.

"A few days ago I visited the Moore House at Yorktown and saw some of the interior. From a young woman living at the house I was able to learn something of its post-Revolutionary history.

"The house and surrounding grounds are owned by Mr. Rockefeller and leased monthly to the occupants who have agreed to evacuate on a sixty day notice. The present house consists of the Colonial structure and some later additions. Previous to 1881 the house had stood vacant for some time, and was once used as a stable. The last extensive repairs were made at the time of the Yorktown Centennial celebration. There is said to be man now living in Yorktown who assisted in the repair work.

"The interior, as it stands, does not exhibit any Colonial work at all. The windows (two light sash) are obviously modern. The roofing is a green asphalt composition. The rear addition is a painful incongruity. Altogether, this building of such great historical association is a great disappointment in its physical appearance.

"I feel that it would be of great value to the Colonial Monument to have this building restored to its probable Revolutionary aspect. The Williamsburg Restoration is the agency eminently equipped to perform such a project. I do not believe that the work could be completed by the time of the Sesquicentennial, but certain obvious mutations of the exterior could be corrected.

(Sgd.) Charles E. Peterson

Jr. Landscape Architect.

P.S. It was noted that this frame structure is protected from fire by a hydrant and hose connected to the Naval Fuel Oil Station tanks. ''

87

APPENDIX NO. 6.

"January 9, 1931.

"Mr. Kenneth Chorley,
     Williamsburg Holding Corporation,
          Williamsburg, Virginia.

Dear Mr. Chorley:

"Copy of a memorandum in regard to the Moore House submitted by Junior Landscape Architect Peterson is inclosed for your information. As we have already advised you, we expect to take over the Moore House property as one of our first land acquisitions at Yorktown. The Urgent Deficiency Bill contains an appropriation of $500,000 for acquisition of lands. The bill also contains $135,000 for administration, maintenance, protection, and improvements. While, or course, most of this is for construction and administration and protection force necessary in connection with the Yorktown Sesquicentennial, there will be some funds for repair and maintenance of buildings. However, this probably would not amount to over $1,000.

"As Peterson points out, it would be of great value to the Colonial Monument to have this building restored to its probable Revolutionary aspect. While we probably could not expect to accomplish this between now and the time of the Sesquicentennial, certain exterior changes could be made. It may be that you have given some thought to this in connection with other restoration work. Any suggestions or cooperation you could extend along this line would be very greatly appreciated.

"Sincerely yours,

(Sgd.) Horace M. Albright

Horace M. Albright, Director."

APPENDIX NO. 7.

"September 21, 1932.

"Memorandum to Mr. Peterson:
REPORT ON EXCAVATIONS AT THE MOORE HOUSE
COLONIAL NATIONAL MONUMENT

"Exploratory excavations were begun upon the grounds of the Moore House during the last week in January, 1932, and carried on with some interruptions until the middle of May. Their purpose was to locate any remaining evidences of outbuildings, walks, or other features which may have existed on the site at the date which will determine the restoration of the grounds—1781. Linked with this was the desirability of exploring further Building No. 2, a part of which was uncovered during the construction of the rear stoop to the present house in the early fall of 1931 and the laying of water pipe at about the same time. In addition, in order to place on record the information thus obtained, drawings were made. These drawings, which accompany this report, are: first, ARCH 1015, a general layout at the scale of 20 feet to the inch showing the present buildings, the topography, and the trenching system (the latter notated), entitled "Plan of Moore House Grounds"; second, ARCH 1010, "Foundation-Building #2" at one-quarter inch to the foot; and third, ARCH 1016, "Building #1" at the same scale.

"Before excavation was begun, study was made of numerous old military maps illustrating the siege of Yorktown, some of which were made shortly after its occurrence. Most of these maps included the area about the Moore House and many of them indicated outbuildings there. Attention was also given to the physical appearance and evidences of the grounds themselves and to typical farm group layouts which we have seen and which suggested further lines of investigation. These studies formed the basis for the system of trenches.

"Observation of the grounds emphasized three things. The well (see 1 on the general drawing) is lined with marl and is apparently old, since the recent use of marl rock has not been common for construction in this section. Depressions, one to the southeast [southwest] in a grove of catalpa trees (see 2) and another roughly opposite to the southwest [southeast] (see 3) were both apparently unnatural.

"Study of the various maps disclosed great dissimilarity in indicated arrangements. Many of these may have been made from memory or very hasty measurements. Some of them were apparently inaccurate in orientation of the buildings; some were copied or adapted from others. The number of outbuildings shown varied from three on the

Bauman Map (American) to nine on the so-called "Rochambeau Map" (French). The completeness of the drawing of the latter lends more credence to it than to most of the others, and while none of them were ignored, the Rochambeau Map became the basis finally for a complete trench layout.

"Working first on the basis of many Tidewater country house plans, an attempt was made to locate at least three outbuildings more or less symmetric to the main house. The southwest depression, excavated to a depth of approximately ten feet, may have been either an ice house or a storage cellar of some sort. No remains of the structure itself were found. At the depth of ten feet there was struck an apparent level, below which the soil was not "fill". This was covered to a depth of several inches with a layer of oyster shells. The pit, as determined by changing soil types is approximately twelve feet in diameter, but is only very roughly circular in plan.

"A grid system, such as is successfully used by the Williamsburg Restoration, was employed to serve as a guide for the trenching. This consisted of a system of rectangular coordinates laid out on the ground with a transit. The guide lines employed are shown on the general drawing. Trenches were dug along these lines two to three or more feet in depth, depending upon the depth of the topsoil and the condition of the subsoil. Digging was begun in the immediate vicinity of the main house and extended outward on all sides. Directly to the rear of the main house were exposed the remains of that known as Building #1 and to the southeast was uncovered the foundation referred to as Building #2.

"These two structures are roughly parallel to each other, but not to the present house. None of the three structures, including the present house, have the same foundation construction, and it seems probable that they were built at three successive intervals. Because Building #2 is the smallest and has a foundation of marl rock, it would appear to be the oldest. The land was patented in 1635. The brick paved floor is at such a low level that it seems probable that it was a basement floor. It would be most unusual if this building were merely a dependency to another to have a large basement fireplace.

"The foundation of Building #2 shows that it was of about the same size as the present house, and since it is so close by, it is probable that the two were never co-existant. There is no indication of any connection. The weakness of the foundations in Building #1 might be accounted for by a log structure in which the marl lined pit might have been either for food or wine storage. It is not impossible that #2 might, after its abandonment as a house, have been used as a kitchen for #1 and perhaps even for the present main house. Most of the maps showed a small structure in about this position.

"Toward the northwest a depression filled with shells, bones, and some brick bats was found (see 4) which would seem to have been merely a "fill". On the north immediately in front of the house was found an irregular area of brick bats, and toward the northeast a smaller irregular area of marl rock. No particular significance is attached to these. They may have been formed during some earlier attempt at levelling the grounds.

"When the immediate vicinity of the house, emphasizing the more promising locations, had been thoroughly covered, trenches were extended to take in the area occupied by buildings shown on the so-called "Rochambeau Map". The earlier trenching had covered as nearly as could be determined by scale all the other maps which, while varying in themselves, could be grouped into several classifications, all of which were investigated. The Rochambeau grouping, an interesting and possible one of nine structures, was transferred to the ground as carefully as possible and excavation made. No results were obtained and nothing found of interest.

"The entire volume of earth enclosed by Building #2 was carefully screened through inch mesh poultry wire arranged on slanting frames, and the material which remained was picked over. Anything of the slightest interest, no matter how modern, was retained and resorted later. The same treatment was employed in the marl lined pit in the corner of Building #1.

"The most usual "find" was broken glass from liquor bottles. In addition, among other articles, there were obtained from Building #1 the following:

"The face, with carved Roman numerals and decoration, two escapement wheels and a cross shaped piece of unknown description, of a clock, all in brass.
The face of a much smaller clock, also in brass.
Several brass buckles of varying shapes.
Several pieces of cabinet hardware of a usual early type, possibly William and Mary or Queen Anne, in brass.
Two pieces of filigree work in brass.
An apothecary's jar, quite small, in china.
Miscellaneous bits of crockery, stoneware, earthenware, glass, china, and ironware. The latter bore several British trademarks.

"From Building #1 were obtained pieces of pottery, china, and ironware, the latter identified as follows:

"Wilkinson & Hulme
Johnson⸺⸺⸺⸺⸺⸺⸺⸺⸺⸺⸺⸺⸺⸺⸺⸺⸺⸺⸺⸺⸺⸺⸺⸺⸺⸺⸺⸺⸺⸺⸺
⸺⸺⸺⸺⸺⸺⸺⸺⸺⸺⸺⸺⸺⸺⸺⸺⸺⸺⸺⸺⸺⸺⸺ogwood & Co.
Maddock (Co?), and others.
Both foundations yielded a good deal of iron, including several keys, a lock face, horse shoes, nails, staples, a bit, a curry comb, and various other items.

"The results in general were disappointing. None of the structures were found which were sought after, nor has any conclusive explanation yet been made to account for those structures and conditions which were found. There are several hypotheses which might explain the failure to find additional structures. The "Gardner" photograph taken during the Civil War indicates that defense earthworks were thrown up upon the grounds. It also shows a structure to the east, possibly a barn and probably not of Colonial origin, of which no trace has been found. The grounds of the Moore House may have suffered during this period as did those of many other houses. This photograph and the "Brady" one taken about the same time reveal the house itself to have been in extremely bad shape. Another consideration is that the structures which might have existed on the grounds in Colonial days to have rounded out even the simplest development might have been of wood on wood foundations and have since disappeared from decay or destruction. It is also possible that, due to lack of more definite information, unknown foundations may still be hidden upon the grounds.

"It was not feasible to carry the exploration further because of the limitation of funds . . . ."

(Signed)

"William M. Haussmann,
Assistant Landscape Architect."

APPENDIX NO. 8

"September 21, 1932.

"Report on Interior Work at the Moore House, January–July, 1932

"I. Exterior and Interior Brickwork at Chimneys.

"A. Repointing, weatherproofing and dampproofing:

"1. The chief source of the dampness occurring in the interior and manifested in discolored and molded plaster was found to be the exterior brickwork. Moisture from the frequent driving rains and seasonal wet spells was admitted in several ways. (1) The handmade brick of which the chimneys are composed is porous, as is all brick except the vitrified variety. Penetration to the interior was possible through porosity. Built largely outside the house, as chimneys of the period frequently were, a large surface was exposed. In addition, the design of the stack provides a wash of flat brick where the successive contractions occur. (2) At these points, and throughout most of the surface, the pointing was found to be in bad condition and to be capable of admitting large quantities of moisture. (3) Where the weatherboarding adjoined the stack, the cement pointing earlier necessitated by shrinkage of the wood had been dislodged and cracked. (4) Where the hip of the roof abutted against the inside of the stack, lack of a suitable cricket prohibited proper drainage and there was consequent seepage of moisture. (5) Since the fireplaces are within, but the flues are without the house, a sloping flue was necessary to connect the one with the other. The upper sides of these flues are directly exposed to the penetration of water from the open top of the chimney.

"2. The Work Done.

Some pointing had been done by others prior to Park Service ownership, but it was found necessary, especially on the broad flanks near the base and on all sides of the T-shaped flue to rake out the joints and repoint them with a good oyster shell lime mortar with some admixture of medium white cement. It was frequently found that a knife blade would penetrate to a depth of several inches. Both stacks were examined

93

with the greatest care from top to bottom and every loose or doubtful joint raked and refilled, especial care being given to the sloping washes. Following this, all new joints were washed when still damp with water in which a very small quantity of mortar and dirt had been dissolved to discolor the new joints. These were laid casually, the lining and tooling being lost occasionally to duplicate the existing work. Following this, the work was washed down with clean water. A cement cricket was built up at the roof line to assist the drainage and the juncture of masonry and weatherboarding carefully repointed. Two coats of Truscon "Super-por-seal" dampproofing—a colorless liquid used for masonry walls above grade—were brushed on in accordance with the manufacturer's specifications. No noticeable alteration in the color or texture of the brickwork was produced.

"On the interior the plaster upon the chimney breasts was entirely removed, and Truscon Plasterbond applied to dampproof the walls to prevent such moisture as may seep through from the open flue to affect the plastered breast. As an additional precaution, the plaster was applied over metal lath.

"Dampers were built into the fireplaces to prevent rain from dropping down onto the hearth and to control the heat of the fire.

"B. Rebuilding Interior Fireplaces:

"1. The Conditions.

"After the plaster had been removed from the chimney breasts in all the rooms, measured drawings to the scale of $1\frac{1}{2}-1'-0''$ were made of them. At the same time careful observations were taken, and photographs made. These were for the purpose of determining the size of the original openings, and revealed the following (See also attached sheet).

"Fireplace A.—Lower left room

"The lining had apparently been patched at various times as the brick burned out. The arch was segmental (as were all), one rowlock course in height, and probably original. About $5'-3''$ from the floor one course of brickwork was recessed $1''$ and may originally have held a means such as a wood lintel for anchoring a mantel. The interior bond was English with closures and probably entirely original except around the fireplace lining. The hearth brick were dry laid and were new common brick. This last was true of all hearths.

"Fireplace B.—Lower right front room

"Much of this opening gave evidence of being original, although about two-thirds of the back and half of the right side had been replaced and the remainder was not in good shape. There were closures at the corners, both on the face and upon the return. On the right to a height of nineteen courses above the floor and running irregularly down to include most of the double rowlock arch were the remains of a kind of red paint, perhaps of clay. Directly above the center of the arch the bond, which elsewhere on the breast was English with closures, was apparently patched and common.

"Fireplace C.—Lower right rear room

"Practically all of the back and half of the sides and jambs had been replaced here. The opening was unusually narrow and one header course to the right of the right side was a vertical line, beyond which the bond exhibited closures, tending to show that the opening had once been a header wider. The dubious character of the shingle rowlock arch and of the brick at the haunches bore out this idea. The fireopening as rebuilt made use of this additional width. Here again across the whole face for a height of nineteen courses were traces of the red paint before referred to. This red area coincided, with the exception of about one foot of width on the extreme right, with common brick bonding. Above the nineteenth course the bond was English. This further tended to prove that the fire opening had been largely rebuilt.

"Fireplace D.—Upper left room

"Here the entire back had been rebuilt, but the sides which in this opening alone were not splayed, were apparently old, though no closures had been used. The crudely built construction above was in bad shape and had largely to be replaced. It was covered with a cement plaster.

"Fireplaces E and F.—Upper right front and rear rooms

"The firebacks were all new brick and some of the sides had been rebuilt. Where the flues receded to the exterior of the house, about eighteen courses from the floor, the breasts continued as a 4″ curtain wall to the ceiling. The right side of F exhibited closures. There were no others occurring as a regular bond. There were traces of plaster on the right side of E. While the brick were apparently handmade, they were poorly laid in commond bond. The breasts bore evidence of patching.

"2. The Rebuilding.

"Handmade brick from a portion of the demolished left wing was cleaned and used as far as possible. In addition, "Jamestowne Collony" brick, handmade by the Pine Dell Company near Five Forks, James City County, Virginia, was used. These replaced the worn linings of all the openings in their sizes as found, with the exception of C, which was widened to its probable original size. The hearths were dry laid in sand in the usual Colonial method. Covert "Old Style" dampers which show no visible operating device from the outside were furnished by the Williamsburg Coal Company and installed. The mortar used both here and for the outside was oyster shell lime with some white cement. The joints were tooled.

"II.   Mantels.

"A. Design:

"1. Condition.

"The existing mantels were obviously Victorian and probably installed when the house was repaired for the Centennial Celebration. On the back of the one in location A was found the pencilled inscription "Colonel Peyton, Yorktown, Va." Colonel Peyton was connected with this work in 1881.

"2. Replacements.

"Mantel A is an adaptation of Colonial motifs in use in Tidewater Virginia prior to the Revolution suitable for a mantel not of the simplest type and is somewhat similar to one installed in the Paradise House at Williamsburg. Mantels B and C, where the fireplaces are back to back, are adaptations of an original one in the Lindsley House at Williamsburg. Their sizes were dictated by the openings which they frame. Mantels D, E, and F follow much simpler precedent, being simple architraves framing the opening. The profile of the moulding was that of the door and window trim which while probably of 1881 installation, is of typical Colonial profile, having possibly at that time been duplicated from some then existant. In E and F, which have precedent in a mantel formerly upstairs and now in the lower left-hand room of the Travis House at Williamsburg, these are capped with a plain shelf. In D the architrave is applied on a backband and the shelf has a simple bed mould. Mantels in the ''Croaker House'' near Norge and at ''Greenwood'' near Culpeper are very similar. Mantels A, B, and C are shown on drawing Col. 1031-C, Sheet 1; D, E, and I on Col. 1031-C. Sheet 2. . . .

''III. Left hand Stair Case.

''1. Condition.

''Leading to the left from the main stair landing was a short run of stairs originally built to give access to the upper floor of the rear wing. The lower floor of this wing was built to serve as a dining room for guests of the Centennial Celebration. The upper floor was added as a bed room by a subsequent occupant, and the stairs cut in at that time. This was corroborated by the discovery of cut joists and studs and the disclosure of some old plaster beneath the newer construction.

''2. Replacement.

''The stairs were removed, joists and flooring laid in the opening, the door casing cut out, studs put on, and lath and plaster on both sides with beaded base boards matching those adjoining. The floor was stained to match that existing, a dark brown in color.

''IV. Doors.

''1. Condition.

''The doors throughout the house were also probably of 1881 installation and undoubtedly of purely Victorian design, as evidenced in the panel design, the locks, and the hinges.

''2. Replacement.

''With the exception of the door to the basement, omitted to reduce costs, the doors throughout were entirely replaced with ones of Colonial design. In order to obtain as much local character as possible, those in the so called ''Sheild House'' built in 1699 were measured and studied. From this basis two types were developed, one for the first and one for the second floor, using the average stile and rail widths and panel proportions and the exact panel moulds as those in the ''Shield House''. Those on the first floor have slightly raised panels, a quarter round on the outside and an ogee panel mould on the inside. The second floor doors are flush paneled and show a quarter round mould on the outside only, there being no mould on the interior. . . . They appear on drawing Col. 1031, Sheet 3.

"V.   Opening Between Front and Rear Right First Floor Rooms

"1. Condition.

"This opening was found with double doors, cased similarly to the others but of much greater width. The doors were designed similar to the others. There was some doubt as to whether an opening of this type would have existed in the structure at the date toward which the Restoration and replacement looked—1781. In consequence plaster and lath around the opening were removed. A heavier stud was found remaining above the opening in such a location as would have made an opening similar in width to the others on the first floor, of the type which was found elsewhere serving as the frame for a doorway, and with a notch in the exact position for a door head. It was a safe assumption that the exigencies of the 1881 Celebration or the Victorian taste had made it seem desirable to widen the opening, and it was decided to restore it to its old width.

"2. Replacement.

"The right-hand casing was retained, the left-hand removed, the door narrowed by the interposition of a new stud and the casing cut down and replaced.

"VI.   Door Hardware.

"1. Condition.

"The replaced doors had been equipped with cast iron butt hinges of a type not known until the beginning of the 19th Century and not commonly used for a decade or two more, and with mortised locks equipped with china knobs, which were unknown in the Revolutionary era.

"2. Replacement.

"The new doors were fitted with H-L hinges duplicated from those in the "Sheild House" . . . and applied with wrought iron "ship" nails whose heads were hammered to produce the old effect. They were located by eye at approximately similar positions to avoid too great regularity. It had been necessary prior to this to replace the sinkages occasioned in the jambs by the putt hinges with old white pins. Surface type black iron "rim" locks with brass knobs and keys, the locks screwed in place, in accordance with the practice of Perry, Shaw and Hepburn in the Williamsburg Restoration, were purchased through the Tom Jones Hardware Company of Richmond, Virginia. . . .

"VII. Partitions at the Rear of the Left-hand First Floor Room.

"1. Condition.

"The exact use to which this room was originally put has not been discovered. The placing of the fireplace in the middle of the end wall made it seem probable that the partitions at the back, noted on the accompanying sketch had at 1781 or prior thereto been non-existent, and that a window might have been similarly located on the right-hand side of the mantel to that now on the left. It was discovered, however, that the two windows on the rear of the house did not balance those on the front. Moreover, because of post-Colonial alterations no trace in the framing of construction or notches for sill or head pieces of a symmetrical window on the chimney wall could be found. The fact that the lathing on the long walls of the room ran completely through the cross partitions was negatived by the knowledge that early construction methods frequently took this course. In addition, much of the lathing on the cross partitions was hand split and applied with wrought nails. It is known that the use of cut nails spread very rapidly after their introduction circa 1800, and that the use of wrought nails practically disappeared soon thereafter. Also the tops of the studs were cut in precisely the same way as were those throughout the remainder of the partitions, of whose age or location there is no question. The location of a door in the short cross wall (2) or on the right facing the rear of the wall (1) was disproved by the complete absence of any evidence therefor. There is some variance in the shaping of the framing members; some are all hewn, some end hewn and side sawn, and some all sawn. The sawing appears to have been all straight cut. Had the studs been erected in 1881, they would probably have been circular sawn. The variance may be explained by different workmen with different tools or in a number of other ways, but does not throw sufficient doubt upon the age of the partitions 1 and 2 to warrant their removal or change.

"2. Replacement

"No change was effected.

'VIII. Plastering and Painting.

"1. Conditions.

"The plaster throughout the house is in bad condition. The wood lath has largely dried out and the key has been broken over large areas. The paint was of the cold water variety and done over in the early fall of 1931, before the Celebration, in some cases too soon over fresh plaster, apparently without sizing, causing it to burn and peel off.

"2. Work done.

"Nothing more than patching was anywhere contemplated, but it became evident as the work progressed that much more both of plastering and painting would have to be done than was originally thought necessary. Demolition of plaster in the weakest areas and elsewhere for inspection disclosed still other areas where it became necessary to cut away to get to a firmer hold. Brushing certain areas for painting revealed other large areas of flaking paint which had to be gone over. The brown and scratched plaster coats were of gypsum plaster, the white coat of lime plaster. Chimney breasts and especially weak areas were metal lathed, all other areas wood lathed. Fresh plaster to be painted was given two coats of size, one before and one after a coat of vinegar designed to neutralize the free alkali. This was followed by a coat of cold water paint matching that already in place. All woodwork was painted with lead and oil paint mixed at the job to match that already existent. The plaster checks of the fireplaces follow Colonial precedent in being painted black. It was not originally intended that they should be plastered since that treatment, although common, was apparently not exclusively adhered to. Although the three mantels on the first floor were produced in accord with the drawings, it was found that minor adjustments in setting would greatly improve their appearance. It was then found advisable to plaster the reveals to cover construction joints.

"Respectfully submitted,

(Sgd.) William M. Haussmann,

Assistant Landscape Architect."

101

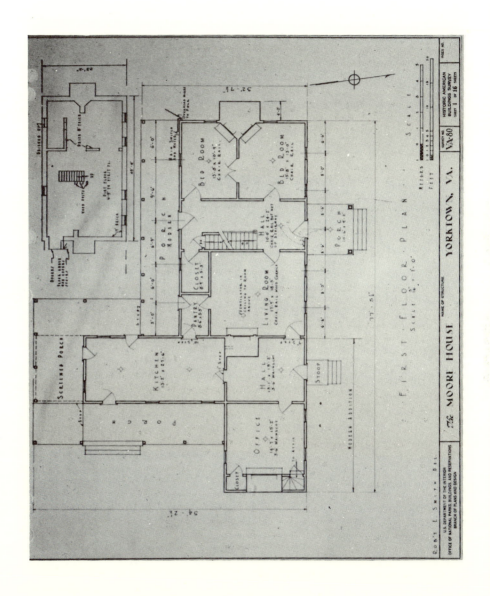

102

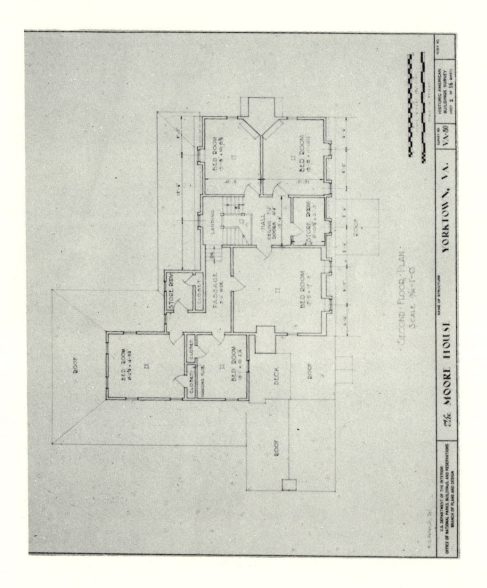

The MOORE HOUSE   YORKTOWN, VA.

Second Floor Plan.
Scale ½=1'-0"

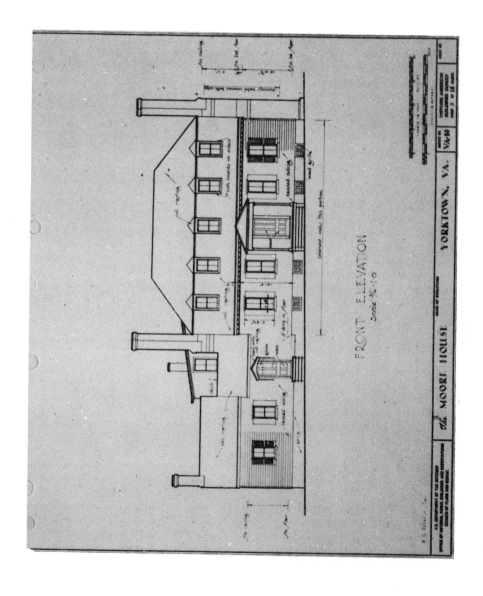

FRONT ELEVATION
Scale ⅜"=1'-0"

The MOORE HOUSE   YORKTOWN, VA.

103

104

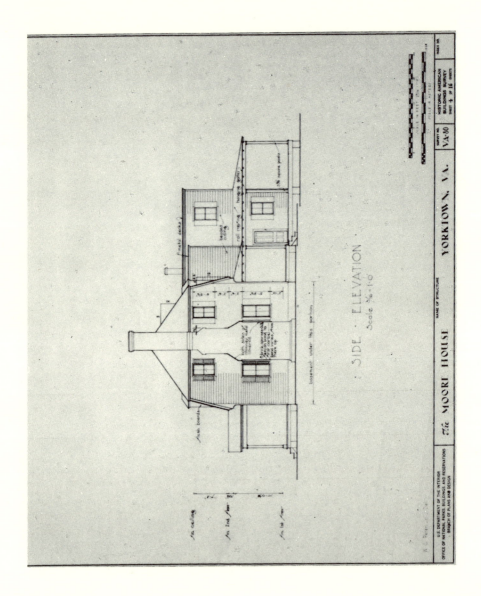

105

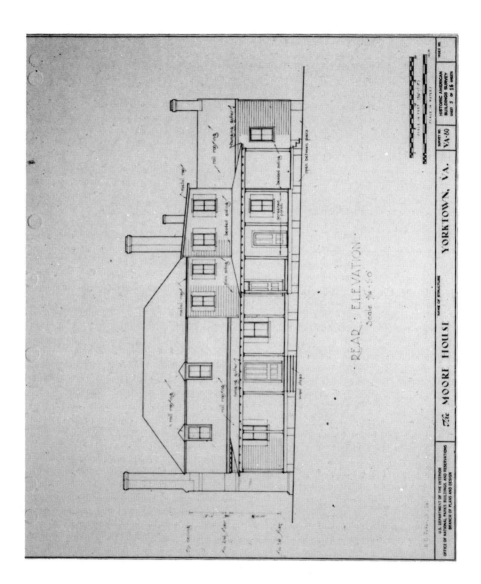

106

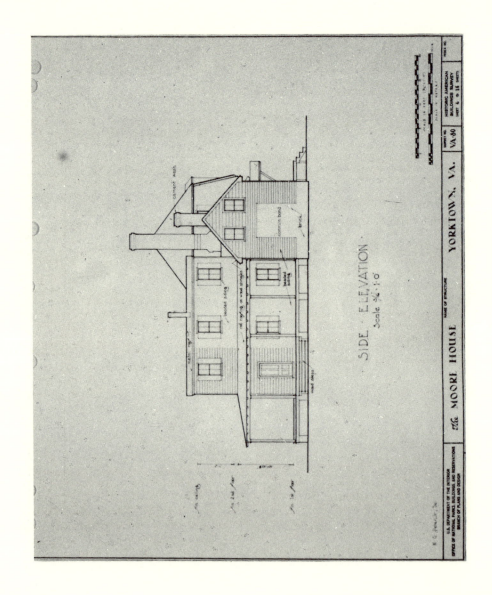

FIRST FLOOR. OFFICE MANTEL.

FIRST FLOOR. FRONT BED ROOM.

FIRST FLOOR. LIVING ROOM MANTEL.

SECTION THRU MANTEL

SECTION THRU MANTEL

SECTION THRU MANTEL

ELEVATION

PLAN

FIREPLACE IN LEFT ROOM ON FIRST FLOOR

The MOORE HOUSE   YORKTOWN, VA.

108

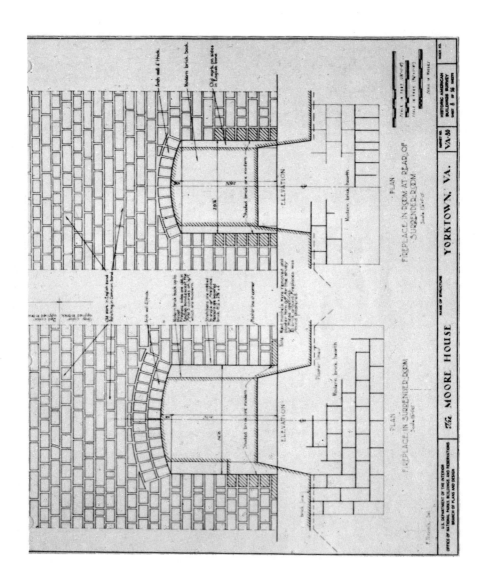

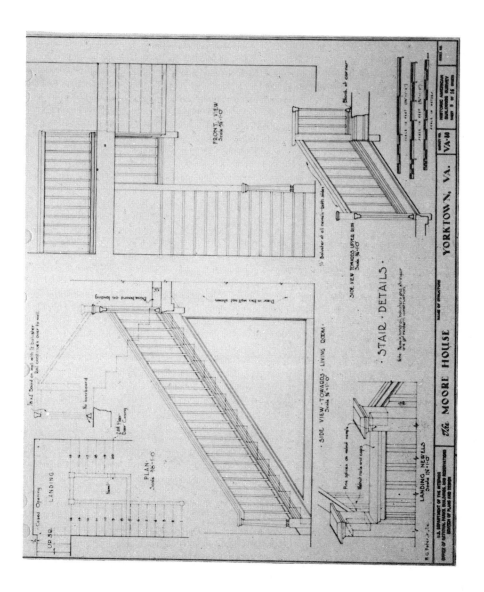

110

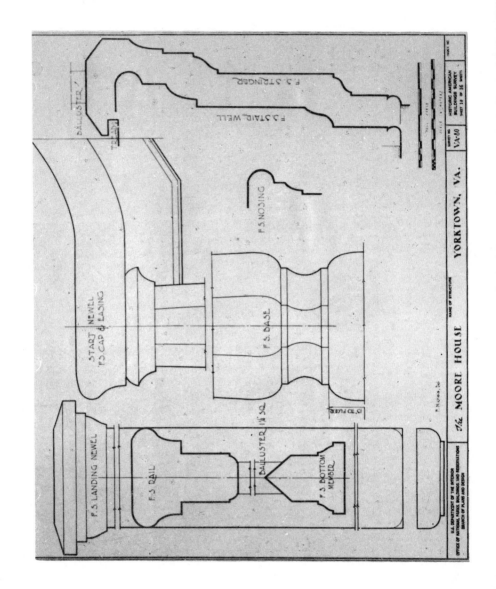

111

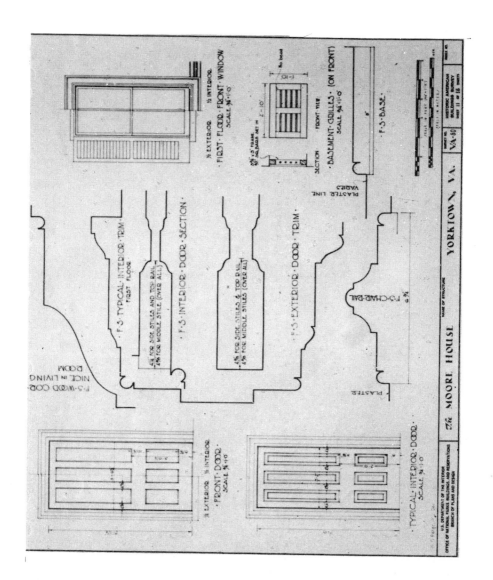

112

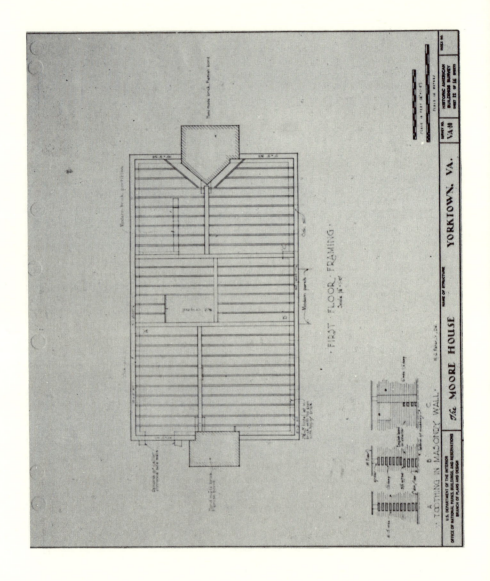

· FIRST FLOOR FRAMING ·

The MOORE HOUSE   YORKTOWN, VA.

· TOOTHING IN MASONRY WALL ·

113

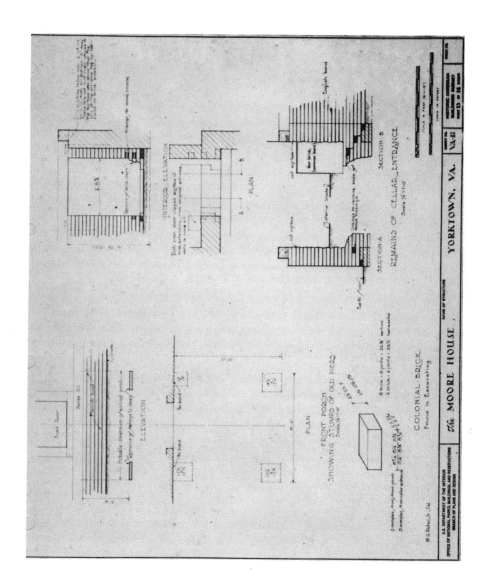

114

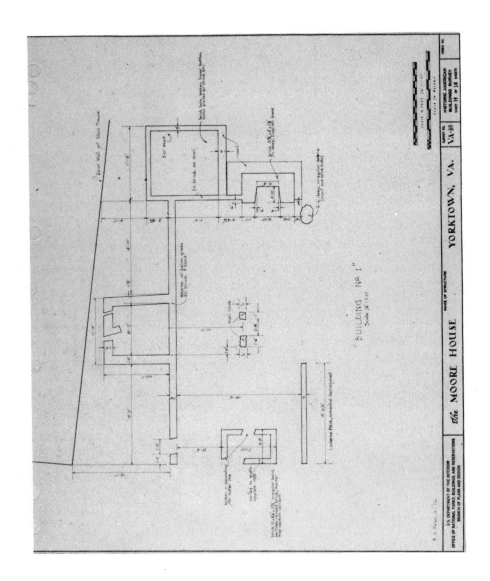

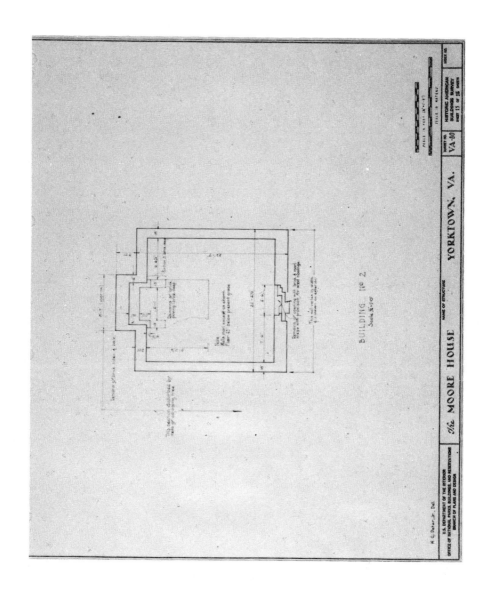

116

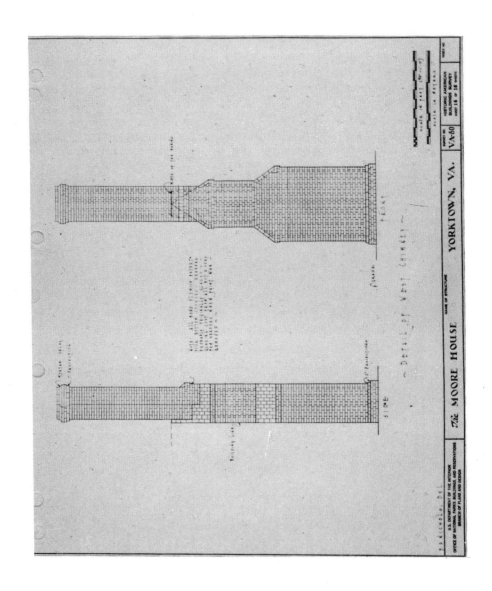